William Garey

Reflected rays of light upon Freemasonry

The Freemason's pocket compendium

William Garey

Reflected rays of light upon Freemasonry
The Freemason's pocket compendium

ISBN/EAN: 9783337270551

Printed in Europe, USA, Canada, Australia, Japan

Cover: Foto ©Andreas Hilbeck / pixelio.de

More available books at **www.hansebooks.com**

THE SCOTTISH

Masonic Calendar

FOR THE

WHOLE OF SCOTLAND,

From the Master Mason to the
33rd Degree.

PRICE, - - SIXPENCE.

POST FREE, - SEVENPENCE.

GEORGE KENNING,

Masonic Publisher,

9 WEST HOWARD STREET, GLASGOW.

THE

Masonic Magazine:

A Monthly Digest of Freemasonry

IN ALL ITS BRANCHES.

Published Monthly, - *Price Sixpence.*

Annual Subscription, 7s.
(Including Postage in the United Kingdom.)

OFFICE:

9 WEST HOWARD STREET,
(Off Jamaica Street,)

GLASGOW.

KENNING'S

CYCLOPÆDIA

OF

FREEMASONRY:

A WORK TREATING FULLY ON

Masonic History and Archæology

UP TO THE PRESENT TIME.

Price 10s. 6d.

GEORGE KENNING,

Masonic Depot,

9 WEST HOWARD STREET,

(Off Jamaica Street),

GLASGOW.

Reflected Rays of Light

UPON

FREEMASONRY;

OR THE

REEMASON'S POCKET COMPENDIUM.

BY

BRO. WM. GAREY,

ABERDEEN.

EDITED BY

BRO. JAMES STEVENSON,

Of "The Freemason's Magazine," and "The Universal Masonic Calendar," Hon. Cor. Mem. Ger. Mas. Union, &c.

With an Emblematical Frontispiece.
FOURTH EDITION.

GEORGE KENNING,

LONDON. { 1, 2 & 3, LITTLE BRITAIN.
175, ALDERSGATE STREET.
198, FLEET STREET.

LIVERPOOL . 2, Monument Place.
GLASGOW . 145, Argyle Street.

Price 1s.; or, post free 1s. 2d. within United Kingdom.
[ENTERED AT STATIONERS' HALL.]
1874.

PREFACE.

IT is with much diffidence and doubt that this little volume is launched on the eddying tide of " Masonic Opinion ;" but the author trusts his zeal for the cause of Freemasonry, and the especial object for which this hand-book is intended, namely, as a preparatory work for the Masonic neophyte, adapted to prepare him for more profound search into the mysteries and teachings of Freemasonry, will be sufficient apology, if any be needed, for the addition of this unassuming contribution to Masonic literature.

In addressing himself to the preparation of the following pages, the author has endeavoured to display the beauties of Freemasonry in as brief, yet comprehensive, and withal in as inexpensive a shape as possible—indeed, he is unaware of any similar work having yet been issued at such a comeatable price, and in so convenient a form—to serve as an unpretentious yet useful Masonic *vade*

mecum. Commending itself not alone to the junior
Masonic student, but also to many Brethren, who,
from their inability to attend at Lodge meetings
and Lodges of Instruction, remain, owing to their
unacquaintance with Masonry, as " Sleeping"
Masons, or " Masonic fungi," to such it is hoped
the present volume may serve as an incentive to
awaken the dormant Brother, direct him in search
of the beautiful inculcations of Masonry, and
stimulate him to become conversant with the various impressive ceremonials of the Order; for his
ultimate improvement must depend upon his own
application and assiduity.

Whilst the ancient landmarks, too, of our Order
have been studiously guarded from the intrusive
gaze of the non-Masonic world, still, to such of the
uninitiated who may chance to peruse the work,
nothing appears but what will show them that our
Order is founded on the purest principles of moral
rectitude.

The exigencies of publishing arrangements have
unavoidably prevented the author attending to
various suggested emendations on the part of
his Editor, but the indulgence of the Brethren is

claimed for the First Edition, which, it is contemplated, will soon be exhausted, and necessitate a second and amended issue of the work.

In addition to the author's gratefulness for the valuable and voluntary co-operation received at the hands of his Editor, Bro. James Stevenson, he has also to return his sincere and grateful thanks to numerous other friends who have assisted him in his labours with their advice, and have afforded him access to various Masonic and other valuable works of reference.

. W. GAREY.

ABERDEEN, *April,* 1869.

THE FIRST DEGREE,

Or, Apprentice.

SYMBOLISM.

THE First or Entered Apprentice Degree is intended to symbolise man, helpless and ignorant, entering into the world ; also youth groping in mental darkness for intellectual light.

QUALIFICATION.

Every Candidate for initiation must believe in the existence of a Supreme Being and future state ; he must be of good moral character, and mature age, and able to conscientiously answer the following questions in the affirmative :—

DECLARATION.

" Do you seriously declare, upon your honour, before these gentlemen, that, unbiassed by friends own inclination, and uninfluenced by

unworthy motives, you freely, and voluntarily
offer yourself a candidate for the mysteries and
privileges of Freemasonry?"

"Do you seriously declare that you are solely
prompted to solicit those privileges, by a favourable
opinion conceived of the Order, a desire of knowledge, and a wish of being more serviceable to your
fellow-creatures?"

"Do you also seriously declare, upon your
honour, that you will cheerfully conform to the
established usages and customs of the Fraternity?"

THE PREPARATION.

" *Oh blindness to the future! kindly given,*
That each may fill the circle marked by Heaven."

The Candidate is required to close his eyes on
the past, and think of the dark mysterious future.
This blindness is emblematical of our ignorance,
and of the Designs of the great Architect of the
Universe being beyond the utmost stretch of the
Human Mind. Yet the study of Nature will
develop intellectual light, dispel ignorance; and
the more it is studied the loftier and more comprehensive will be our ideas of the **Great Creator**
and First Cause of all things.

" *Nature is but a name for an effect,*
Whose cause is God."

Equality.—As Masonry does not regard, or
admit any person on account of rank or fortune,
he should divest his mind of all selfish and worldly
considerations, and lay aside the trinkets and
trappings of the outward world, and for a time
become poor and penniless; so that he may
remember, when asked to assist a Brother in distress, that Masonry received him in poverty, and

that he should then embrace the opportunity of practising that virtue, Charity,

> " *Which is the spirit that, with widest plan,*
> *Brother to brother binds, and man to man.*"

His **Sincerity** of purpose and purity of mind are symbolised by the left breast being made bare ;— in token of implicit, or unreserved **Confidence,** the right arm is uncovered ; so also in token of **Humility** is the left knee made bare, to bend before the Great Author of his existence ; and to follow the ancient custom of the Israelites, he will be prepared to slip the shoe from off his foot, as a testimony or token of **Fidelity** (Ruth iv. 7). The Cable Tow, with a running noose, is emblematical of the Dangers which surround us in this life, especially if we should stray from the paths of duty. It will also remind the initiated to submit, while he is in ignorance, to being guided by those whom he knows to be enlightened.

> " *Convince the world that you're devout and true,*
> *Be just in all you say, in all you do.*"

THE INITIATION.

" Ask and it shall be given you; seek, and you shall find; knock, and it shall be opened unto you."—MATT. vii. 7.

The knocks at the door denote Peace, Harmony, and Brotherly Love. Before the ceremony of Initiation begins, the Candidate is informed that Freemasonry is an institution founded on the purest principles of Morality—*i.e.*, on Truth, Brotherly Love, and Charity ; and requires a cheerful compliance, to maintain the established usages and customs of the Order. The moment we enter the world, and draw the first breath of life, the Sword of Justice is pointed to our heart, and will sooner or later overtake us ; so in Masonry, at our first entrance we are taught to be cautious, and trust in God.

Prayer.—Vouchsafe Thine aid, Almighty Father, and Supreme Architect of the Universe, to this our present convention ; and grant this Candidate for Masonry may dedicate and devote his life to Thy service, so as to become a true and faithful Brother among us. Endow him with a competency of Thy Divine Wisdom, that, assisted by the lessons of our Moral Science, he may be better enabled to display the beauties of Godliness, to the Honour and Glory of Thy Most Holy Name. (So mote it be.) Amen.

THE PILGRIMAGE.

Where the blessing of God is invoked, the candidate may fear no danger, but arise, and follow his enlightened guide, who will enable him to travel safely through the dark emblematic pilgrimage of ignorance, and overcome the obstructions and difficulties which beset the way of knowledge.

This part of the ceremony symbolises the progress of human intelligence, from a state of ignorance, to the highest state of civilisation and mental enlightenment. During the time of this part, in some lodges the 133rd Psalm is read, to impress the Candidate and Brethren with a feeling of Brotherly Love.

> " *Perfect love has power to soften*
> *Cares that might our peace destroy,*
> *Nay, does more—transforms them often,*
> *Changing sorrow into joy.*"

Or the following may be sung with good effect—

Tune—" Artaxerxes."

" *Behold ! how pleasant and how good*
  For brethren such as we,
Of the accepted brotherhood,
  To dwell in unity.
' *Tis like the oil on Aaron's head,*
  Which to his feet distills ;
Like Hermon's dew so richly shed,
  On Zion's sacred hills !

For there the Lord of light and love,
  A blessing sent with power ,
Oh, may we all this blessing prove,
  E'en life for evermore !
On Friendship's altar, rising here,
  Our hands now plighted be,
To live in love, with hearts sincere,
  In peace and unity.

The hand placed on the Bible will remind us of the obligations we owe to God and our fellow-men.

THE SECRECY AND VOWS OF FIDELITY.

" *Heaven from all creatures hides the book of fate,*
  All but the page prescribed, their present state."

Having completed the symbolic journey in search of enlightenment, Vows of Fidelity or Secrecy are required ; but these are voluntary, and the Candidate must be assured, previous to his taking them, that there is nothing in those Vows incompatible with his civil, moral, or religious duties. The Veil of Secrecy which shrouds Freemasonry has attracted the attention of the uninitiated more than anything else ; and by their conjectures, have attributed to it many erroneous notions, some of which, none but the most ignorant could believe—such as using incantations, and raising unearthly-like beings, or performing some waggish mischief on the Candidate. The writer has often seen a Candidate enter the Lodge trembling with fear, and has known of others, who, after being partly prepared, became so suspicious or afraid of some evil, that they would not proceed, even though assured by members of the contrary. But some may naturally reason in their own mind :—"If the objects and pretensions of Freemasonry be honest and praiseworthy, what need is there for an obligation to secrecy? If it be really a system of morality, and have a tendency to elevate the mind, or be a benefit to mankind, why not make it free to all? And charity being boasted of as one of its characteristic features, is it not Masons' bounden duty, as charitable men, to make it known without fee or price, instead of binding the members by fearful oaths to secrecy?" The only answer which we can give to these questions is, That nature is shrouded in mystery ; and mystery has charms for all men. Whatever is familiar to us, however novel, beautiful, or elevating, is often disregarded, unnoticed, or despised ; whilst novelty, however trifling or devoid of intrinsic value, will charm and captivate the imagination, and become the fuel of curiosity, which cannot bear to be ignorant of what others know. And so Freemasonry, taking the example of Nature, veils its beauties in mystery, and illustrates them by symbols. In support of this, we will conclude this part by quoting two distinguished modern writers :—

" Thoughts will not work, except in silence ; neither will virtue work, except in secrecy. . Like other plants, virtue will not grow, unless its roots be hidden, buried from the light of the sun. Let the sun shine on it—nay, do but look at it privily thyself—the roots wither, and no flowers will glad thee."— *Thomas Carlyle, " Sartor Resartus."*

"God has put the veil of secrecy before the soul for its preservation ; and to thrust it rudely aside, without reason, would be suicidal. Neither here, nor, as I think, hereafter, will our thoughts and feelings lie open to the world."—*H. W. Beecher, " Life Thoughts."*

THE ENLIGHTENMENT.

"The light shineth in darkness ; and the darkness comprehendeth it not."—JOHN 1. 5.
"And God said, let there be light, and there was light."—GEN. 1. 3.

This particular part of the ceremony symbolises the victory of Knowledge over Ignorance, and the impression intended to be made on the mind of the Candidate on first beholding the Three Great Lights of Masonry, is to make him recollect that the light of Wisdom is beautiful, and that all her paths are peace.

" ' *Tis the Great Spirit, wide diffused
   Through everything we see,
   That with our spirits communeth
   Of things mysterious—life and death,
   Time and Eternity !*

" The people that walked in darkness have seen a great light : they that dwell in the land of the shadow of death ; upon them hath the light shined." —ISAIAH ix. 2.

THE ***** ***** ******

Are the Holy Bible,* Square, and Compasses.
The Bible to govern our faith and practice, being
the gift of God to man for that purpose ; the
Square to regulate our actions ; and the Compasses to keep us in due bounds with all mankind.

THE ****** ******

Are three burning Candles or Tapers, emblematical of the Spirit of God, whereby His chosen people
are enlightened, and are also meant to represent, the
Sun to rule the day, the Moon to rule the night,
and the Master to rule and govern his Lodge with
equal regularity.   They are also emblematical of
the Master and his Wardens, and are placed in
the east, south, and west ; as the sun rises in
the east, so the Worshipful Master is placed in
the east, to open his lodge, and enlighten his
brethren in Masonry.

The Junior Warden represents the sun at its
meridian in the south, and as it is then the beauty
and glory of the day, it is his duty to call the
brethren from labour to refreshment, see that they
do not convert the time thereof into intemperance,
but to regulate them so that pleasure and profit
may be enjoyed by all.

The Senior Warden represents the sun in the
west at the close of the day, and it is his duty to
see that the Brethren are all satisfied, and that they
have had their just dues, before closing the lodge
by command of the Master.

THE SECRETS.

Having been converted into one of the Sons of

* But in countries where it is not known, any other book, or emblem, which is understood to contain the Will of God.

Light, and taught to be cautious, the Candidate may be intrusted with the Secrets belonging to this degree, which consist of a Sign, a Grip or Token, and a Word. For these the reader is referred to the lodge-room; but it would be well to remember that all squares, levels, and upright lines allude to the Obligation, and are proper signs by which to know a Mason.

THE INVESTITURE.

After the reciprocal communication of the marks which distinguish us as Masons, the Candidate is invested with a lambskin or white apron. It is the Emblem of Innocence, the Badge of a Mason, and the Bond of Brotherhood; and, when worthily worn as such, will give pleasure to himself and honour to the fraternity; and be of more value than the diadems of Kings. or the pearls of Princesses; and it should remind him that purity of life and rectitude of conduct are necessary to gain admission to the Celestial Lodge, where the Supreme Architect presides.

CHARGE AFTER INVESTITURE

You are never to put on that Badge if you are at variance with any Brother in the lodge; if so, either or both of you must retire, so that the harmony of the assembly be not disturbed by your unseemly strife. When haply your differences are reconciled, you may return and clothe yourselves, and "dwell together in unity," for brotherly love is regarded as the strongest cement of the Order.

THE FOUNDATION STONE

Of every masonic edifice is, or ought to be, placed in the north-east corner of the building;

and the newly initiated Brother is made to represent that stone, and there receives his first lesson on Moral Architecture, teaching him to walk and act uprightly before God and man ; as well as for special reasons, a striking illustration of brotherly love and charity, which he is unable, in his present condition, to bestow (1 Kings vi. 7). But charity is the principal of all social virtues, and the distinguishing characteristic of Masons. Let the feelings of the heart, guided by reason, direct the hand of Charity :—

" *When the fleet vanities of life's brief day*
  Oblivion's hurrying wing shall sweep away ;
Each act by Charity and Mercy done,
  High o'er the wrecks of time shall live alone."

THE WORKING TOOLS

Are the twenty-four inch Gauge, the common Gavel, and the Chisel. Their use in operative Masonry is obvious, and requires no explanation ; but as speculative or Free Masons, we see them applied to our morals, thus—

THE TWENTY-FOUR INCH GAUGE

Is emblematical of the twenty-four hours of the day, which ought to be devoted to the service of God by a proper division of our time, for prayer, labour, refreshment, and sleep.

THE COMMON GAVEL

Is the emblem of Reason, and of labour being the lot of man. By reasoning and examining ourselves, we see the necessity of breaking off and divesting our consciences of all vice, thereby fitting our minds, as living stones, for that spiritual building eternal in the heavens.

" Vice is a monster of so frightful mein,
As, to be hated, needs but to be seen."

THE CHISEL

Is the emblem of Perseverance, which is necessary to establish perfection, promote the habit of
virtue, enlighten the mind, and make the soul
pure. Education gives polish to the mind, as the
chisel by perseverence gives smoothness to the
stone.

THE JEWELS

Of a lodge arè Six in number—viz., three
movable and three immovable. The three movable are the Square, Level, and Plumb ;* the three
immovable are the Rough Ashler, the Perfect
Ashler, and the Trestle Board.†

THE ROUGH ASHLER

Represents man in his natural state, ignorant,
unpolished, and vicious, like a precious stone surrounded by a dense crust, its beauty unseen till
the rough surface is removed.

THE PERFECT ASHLER

Represents him in a high state of civilisation,
with his mind divested of all vice, and prepared
for that house, not made with hands, eternal in
the heavens, which, by a liberal and virtuous education, our own endeavours, and the grace of God,
we hope to attain.

* The Square, Level, and Plumb being the working tools in the
Second Degree, are explained at page 24
† In America, the reverse is the case, the immovable being the
Square, Level, and Plumb, because always found in the east, south,
and west,

THE TRESTLE BOARD

Represents the Book of Life, or Natural and Revealed Religion, in which the Supreme Architect of the Universe has drawn designs to guide us, and laid down precepts whereby we are to erect our spiritual temple, and find acceptance into the city of our God.

THE THREE VIRTUES

Of an Entered Apprentice are symbolically designated the Precious Jewels, which are, in this Degree, an Attentive Ear, a Silent or Instructive Tongue, and a Faithful Heart.

AN ATTENTIVE EAR

Is to be given to the instructions of your superiors in knowledge, and the calls of a worthy, distressed Brother. All nature, and the events which are continually happening in the world's history, proclaim lessons of wisdom which an attentive ear will remember. But there are many entering the porch of Masonry, who, for want of this virtue, fall asleep in the arms of indolence, and do not penetrate beyond the surface, to find the golden treasures which the rich mine contains.

A SILENT TONGUE

Is the sanctuary of Prudence and Discretion. This virtue is essential to Masons, so that the vail of Mystery behind which our secrets are hidden may not be incautiously drawn aside. It will also remind us that we should "Speak evil of no man," and that it is more honourable to vindicate than to accuse. Whom we cannot approve, we should pity in silence. Titus, chap. iii.

A FAITHFUL HEART

To fulfil your obligations, is the safest repository in which you can lock up your secrets, and exemplify your Honour and Fidelity.

CHALK, EARTH, AND CHARCOAL

Are emblematical of Freedom, Fervency, and Zeal, which are qualifications necessary to promote independence, devotion, and love in the heart of every faithful servant. "There is nothing freer than chalk, the slightest touch of which leaves a trace behind; no heat more fervent than burning charcoal; and nothing more zealous than the earth to bring forth." We must love God with freedom, fervency, and zeal.

BROTHERLY LOVE, RELIEF, AND TRUTH

Are the three great Tenets or Principles of a Freemason.

BROTHERLY LOVE

Is the strongest cement of the Order, and without it the Fraternity would soon cease to exist. By it we are taught to regard the whole human species as one family, to aid, support, and protect each other.

RELIEF

Flows from brotherly love, and it is a duty incumbent on all men, to soothe the unhappy, relieve the distressed, and restore peace to their troubled minds.

TRUTH

Is a divine attribute, and the mother of Virtue; and the first lesson we are taught in Masonry is to be fervent and zealous in the pursuit of truth, and to dispense it freely.

THE LODGE-ROOM

Is a representation of the world; and a properly constructed lodge should be situated due east and west, for which we assign three Masonic reasons—First, the sun rises in the east, and sets in the west; second, Learning originated in the east, and extended to the west; third, The Tabernacle in the Wilderness was so situated (Exodus, chaps. xxvi. and xxvii.), to commemorate the miraculous east wind (Exodus xiv. 21), and being symbolic of the universe, was the type of a Freemason's Lodge.

ITS FORM,

Being an oblong square, or double cube, is emblematical of the united powers of Darkness and Light.

ITS DIMENSIONS

Embrace every clime; in length, from east to west; in breadth, between the north and south; in depth, from the surface of the earth to the centre; and in height, from earth to heaven; denoting the universality of its influence.

WISDOM, STRENGTH, AND BEAUTY

Are the three great pillars on which the Lodge-room is supported. Wisdom to contrive, govern, and instruct; Strength to support; and Beauty to adorn. The W. M. in the east represents Wisdom, the S. W. in the west represents Strength, and the J. W. in the south represents Beauty. Their situations forming a triangle is emblematical of their unity in forming one Government ; they also represent Solomon, King of Israel, for his wisdom ; Hiram, King of Tyre, for his assistance in building the Temple ; and Hiram Abiff, for his cunning or beautiful workmanship. These three great pillars are represented by the three principal orders of Architecture, *i.e.*, the Doric, Ionic, and Corinthian. The Ionic column represents Wisdom, because it wisely combines strength with grace. Strength is represented by the Doric, being the strongest and most massive of the orders. Beauty is represented by the Corinthian, being the most beautiful and ornamental.

THE COVERING

Of a Freemason's Lodge is the Celestial Canopy, or the starry decked Heavens,

> " *Where streams of joy glide ever on,*
> *Around the Lord's eternal throne.*"

The sun, moon, and stars are emblems of God's power, goodness, omnipresence, and eternity.

THE FURNITURE

Consists of the Holy Bible, Square, and Compasses. The Bible is the symbol of God's Will, and is dedicated to His service ; the Square to the Master, being the emblem of his office ; the Compasses are dedicated to the whole Craft, being emblematical of the limits which ought to circumscribe our conduct, that we may live with honour, and be respected by a large circle of good friends, and make our exit from the stage of life in the humble hope of being rewarded with a Crown of Glory.

THE ORNAMENTS

Are the Mosaic Pavement, the Indented Border, and Blazing Star.

THE MOSAIC PAVEMENT

Reminds us of the bounteous liberality of our Father in heaven, who has spread the earth with a beauteous carpet, and wrought it, as it were, in Mosaic work. It also represents the world chequered over with good and evil, pain and pleasure, grief and joy : to-day we walk in prosperity, to-morrow we totter in adversity ; but, united in the Bond of Brotherhood, and walking uprightly, we may not stumble.

THE INDENTED BORDER

Of the Mosaic Carpet may be likened to the wavy ocean, which skirts the land, and by indenting it, adds beauty to the earth ; but it is emblematically intended to represent the many blessing and comforts with which we are surrounded in thi life, but more especially those which we hope to enjoy hereafter.

THE BLAZING STAR

Is the emblem of Prudence, which should shine conspicuous in our conduct, and be the guiding star of our lives, instructing us to regulate our actions by the dictates of reason and experience, to judge wisely, and determine with propriety, on everything that tends to our present or future happiness. Its proper place is in the centre of the lodge, so as to be ever present to the eye, that the heart may be attentive to the dictates, and steadfast in the laws of Prudence.

THE TASSELS

Which adorn the four corners of the Indented Border, are emblematical of the Cardinal Virtues —viz., Prudence, Fortitude, Temperance, and Justice. (For Prudence see the " Blazing Star.")

FORTITUDE

Is that virtue which enables us to bear the adversities of social life, encounter danger, resist temptation, and keep us in the practice of Virtue.

TEMPERANCE

Sets bounds to our desires, frees the mind from the allurements of vice, and renders our passions tame and governable. The health of the body, and the dignity of man, depend upon a faithful observance of this virtue.

JUSTICE

Is the boundary of Right, and the cement of Civil Society. Without the exercise of this virtue, social intercourse could not exist ; might would usurp the place of right, and universal confusion ensue. Justice commands you to " Do unto others as you would that others should do unto you." Let Prudence direct you, Fortitude support you, Temperance chasten you, and Justice be the guide of all your actions.

THE THEOLOGICAL LADDER,

Which Jacob saw in his vision, extending from earth to heaven, represents the way of salvation, the many steps composing it representing as many moral virtues, the principal being Faith, Hope, and Charity. It rests on the volume of the Sacred Law,

2

which strengthens our Faith, and creates Hope in Immortality ; but Charity is the chief of all social virtues, and the distinguishing characteristic of the Order ; and the Mason possessed of that virtue in its widest sense, may be said to wear the brightest jewel that can adorn the Fraternity. The Sacred Volume is represented on the Tracing Board as resting on the vortex of a circle, which is em-bordered by two perpendicular parallel lines, re-presenting Moses and King Solomon ; or (in Christian Lodges) St. John the Baptist and St. John the Evangelist, who, in Masonry, it is under-stood, were parallels, and exemplary of those virtues which Masons are taught to reverence and practise.

THE CIRCLE

Represents the Boundary Line of a Mason's conduct ; and in going round the circle, we neces-sarily touch upon these lines, and the Holy Scrip-tures, which point out the whole duty of man ; and they who circumscribe their conduct by those examples, and the precepts therein contained, cannot materially err. There is a point within the circle referring to the Glorious Throne of God, the Great Architect and Creator of the Universe, who is Almighty, of infinite Wisdom, and whose Being extends through boundless space, enjoying alone the attributes of Immortality and Eternity ! This symbol of God is almost universal in his works.

The God of Nature and of Grace
  In all his works appears ;
His goodness through the earth we trace,
  His grandeur in the spheres.

THE LEWIS,

Which is dovetailed into the Perfect Ashler, denotes Strength, to support us in all our lawful undertakings. It also denotes the son of a Mason, whose duty it is to support his aged parents, when they are unable to labour or bear the burden of cares, gathered upon them in their journey through life.

CHARGE TO NEWLY ADMITTED BRETHREN.

You have now passed through the ceremony of your Initiation, and been admitted a member of our ancient and honourable Order. Knowledge and virtue are the objects of our pursuit ; and the Great Architect of the Universe is our Supreme Master. On him we rely for support and protection, and to his will we ought to submit, while we work by the unerring rule he has given to guide us. By having said so much, we do not mean you to understand that Masons arrogate to themselves everything that is great, good, and honourable. By no means. The gates of knowledge, and the paths of truth and virtue, are open to all who choose to enter and walk therein ; but this much may be affirmed of Masonry, that the moral lessons which it teaches favour us with peculiar advantage, which, if duly studied and practised, would exalt us above the rest of mankind

As a Mason, you are bound to be a strict observer of the moral law, as contained in the Holy Writings, and to consider these as the unerring standard of Truth and Justice, and by their divine precepts, to regulate your life and actions. Therein is inculcated your duly to God, your neighbour, and yourself ; to God, in never mentioning his name but with that reverential awe which becomes a creature to bear to his Creator, and to look upon him as the source of all good, which we came into the world to enjoy, to love, and obey; to your neighbours, by acting on the Square, and doing unto them as you would wish them to do unto you; to yourself, in avoiding all irregularity and intemperance, or debasing your dignity as a man, and a Mason. A zealous attachment to these duties will insure public and private esteem.

As a citizen, you should be exemplary in the discharge of your civil duties, true to your government, and just to your country, yielding obedience to the laws which afford you protection.

As an individual, be careful to avoid reproach or censure; let not interest, favour, or prejudice bias your integrity, or influence you to be guilty of any dishonourable action; and, above all, practise benevolence and charity, so far as you can without injury to yourself or family. But do not suppose that Masonry confines your good offices to the Fraternity only, or absolves you from your duty to the rest of mankind,—it inculcates Universal Benevolence, and extends its benign influence to the whole world. Your frequent attendance at our meetings we earnestly solicit, yet it is not meant that Masonry should interfere with your necessary avocations; but in your leisure time, that you may improve in Masonic Knowledge, you should converse with well informed Brethren, who will be as ready to give as you to receive instruction. Finally, you are to keep sacred and inviolable the mysteries of the Order, as these are to distinguish you from the rest of the community; and if a person of your acquaintance is desirous of being initiated into Masonry, be careful not to recom-

mend him, unless you are convinced he will conform to our rules, that the honour and reputation
of the Institution may be firmly established.

Your attention to this charge will lead us to
hope that you will estimate the real value of Freemasonry, and imprint on your mind the dictates of
TRUTH, HONOUR, AND JUSTICE.

THE SECOND DEGREE,
Or, Fellow Craft.

" The summer shall ripen what the spring began,
  Youth's generous fires shall glow more fervent in the man."

IN the pursuit of Knowledge, the intellectual faculties are employed in promoting the glory of God, and the good of man. In this Degree, the young Mason is represented as having attained the age of Manhood, and labouring to overcome the difficulties which beset him in the attainment of the hidden mysteries of learning and science, to which he is introduced and enjoined to study, so that he may see knowledge rising out of its first elements, and be led, step by step, from simple ideas, through all the windings and labyrinths of Truth, to the most exalted discoveries of the human Intellect.

PRAYER AT OPENING.

Oh God, Grand Geometrician, and Master of the Universe, we implore thee to cause the Light of thy Divine Wisdom to shine upon us, and enlighten the dark ignorance of our souls, so that we may view the beauties of thy handiwork, and comprehend more fully thy almighty power and goodness.

> " *Such blessings from thy gracious hand,*
> *Our humble prayers implore :*
> *And thou shalt be our chosen God,*
> *And portion evermore.*"   *Amen.*

THE WORKING TOOLS

Of this Degree are the Square, Level, and Plumb.

THE SQUARE

In this Degree is a very important instrument, as none can become a Fellow Craft without its assistance. It is the emblem of Morality and Virtue, reminding us to square our actions, and harmonise our conduct by the unalterable principles of the moral law as contained in the Holy Bible, and we are obligated to act upon the Square with all mankind, but especially with our Brethren in Masonry.

THE LEVEL

Is the emblem of Equality, and reminds us that we are descended from the same stock, partake of the same nature, and share the same hope. In the sight of God all men are equal ; and the time will come when all distinctions but that of goodness shall cease, and Death, the grand leveller of human greatness, reduce us all to the same state.

THE PLUMB

· Is the emblem of Justness and Uprightness, and admonishes us to hold the scales of Justice in equal poise, and make our conduct coincide with the line of our duty, which is to walk uprightly before God and man.

THE JEWELS.

The Three Symbolic or precious Jewels of a Fellow Craft are Faith, Hope and Charity.

FAITH IN GOD.

" *For humble Faith, with steadfast eye,*
  Points to a brighter world on high."

HOPE IN IMMORTALITY.

" *Daughter of Faith! Awake, arise, illume*
  The dread unknown, the Chaos of the tomb."

CHARITY TO ALL MANKIND

" *Secures her votaries unblasted fame,*
  And in celestial annals 'graves their name."

THE SABBATH

Should be regarded by every good Mason with reverence, being instituted by God as a day of rest and devotion,

" *To spread the page of Scripture, and compare*
  Our conduct with the laws engraven there."

THE TWO PILLARS OF BRASS,

Which were placed at the porch or entrance to King Solomon's Temple, are described in 1 Kings vii. 15-22, 2 Kings xxv. 17, Jer. lii. 21-23, as being eighteen cubits high; but, in 2 Chron. iii. 15-17, they are said to have been "thirty and five cubits high." This discrepancy is supposed to have arisen by the aggregate height of both Pillars being given in Chronicles, and allowing half a cubit of each to be hidden in the joining holes of the Chapiters. The Chapiters on the top were of molten brass, and five cubits in height. Although another discrepancy seemingly exists in 2 Kings xxv. 17, where it is said that they were only three cubits, but if we allow two cubits for the " wreathen work and pomegranates" described, they will amount to five cubits. The net work denotes Unity; the lily work, Peace; and the pomegranates, from the exuberance of their seed, Plenty. The Chapiters were also surmounted by two pommels or globes (1 Kings vii. 41 ; 2 Chron. iv. 12), which, according to Masonic tradition, were the archives of Masonry, and contained the maps and charts of the celestial and terrestial bodies, denoting the universality of Masonry, and that a Mason's charity should be equally extensive, bounded only by Prudence, and ruled by Discretion, so that real want and merit may be relieved, and the knave prevented from eating the bread which Virtue in distress ought to have. Pillars of such magnitude, strength, and beauty could not but attract the attention of those who beheld them, and impress upon their minds the idea of strength and stability which their names imply, and will be remembered by every Mason. The destruction of these immense pillars, the magnificent temple, and city, is significant of the weakness and instability of human greatness, and th at our strength can only be in God; and faith in h.im is the only foundation on which we can build our future temple of happiness to stand firm for ever. 2 Sam. xii. 17 ; 1 Kings ix. 3-7.

THE WINDING STAIR.

Having passed the pillars of the porch, the Candidate, seeking for more light by the mysteries contained in the Second Degree, must approach the east by a supposed Winding Stair, symbolically leading from the ground floor to the Middle Chamber of Masonry. The only reference to it in scripture is in 1 Kings vi. 8.

Before entering the Middle Chamber, where as Masons, we are told that the Fellow Craft went to receive their wages, they had to give a certain password, in proof that they were not imposters. This password was instituted at the time when Jephtha put the Ephraimites to flight, and slew forty and two thousand at the different fords and passes of the river Jordan (Judges xii. 1-7). The word *Shibboleth* means the ford of a river, or an ear of corn, and is depicted on the Tracing Board by an ear of corn near a stream of water ; but, as speculative Masons, it is the lesson which this symbol is intended to illustrate that we have to consider, for, by historical facts and natural reasons, we cannot suppose that the legend as rehearsed in the lodge-room is anything more than a philosophical myth. Masonic Symbolism shows the Candidate as always rising towards a higher state of perfection. In the first degree, we have the Theological Ladder, impressing this idea ; in the Second Degree, we have the Winding Staircase, symbolising the laborious ascent to eminence in the attainment of the hidden mysteries of learning and science. The Symbolic Staircase is composed of three, five, seven, or other unequal number of steps.

THE THREE STEPS represent youth, or the Degree of the Entered Apprentice, viz.—1st, his being born to Masonic life ; 2nd, his ignorance of the world in his childhood ; 3rd, the lessons which he receives in his youth to prepare his mind for the instruction which is given in the succeeding Degrees; they also allude to the three supports, Wisdom, Strength, and Beauty.

THE FIVE STEPS allude to Manhood, or the Fellow Craft Degree, the Five Orders of Architecture, and the Five Human Senses.

THE SEVEN STEPS refer to Old Age, or the Third Degree; the seven Sabbatical Years, seven Years of Famine, seven Golden Candlesticks, seven Planets, seven Days of the Week, seven Years in Building the Temple, seven Wonders of the World, &c., but more especially to the seven liberal Arts and Sciences. The total number of Steps, amounting in all to Fifteen, is a significant symbol, for fifteen was a sacred number among the Orientals, because the letters of the holy name JAH, יה, were, in their numerical value, equivalent to fifteen; the Fifteen Steps of the Winding Stair are therefore symbolic of the name of God; and hence a figure, in which the nine digits were so disposed as to count fifteen either way when added together perpendicularly, horizontally, or diagonally, constituted one of their most sacred talismans.

15	15	15	15
15	8	1	6
15	3	5	7
15	4	9	2
15			

Masons are indebted for the symbol of odd numbers to Pythagoras, who considered them more perfect than even ones; therefore, odd numbers predominate in Masonry, and are intended to symbolise the idea of perfection. In ancient times it was considered a fortunate omen, when ascending a stair, to commence with the right foot, and find the same foot foremost at the top; and this is said to be the reason why ancient temples were ascended by an odd number of steps.

It is then as a symbol, and a symbol only, that we study the legend of the Winding Staircase ; to adopt it as an historical fact, the absurdity of its details stares us in the face. What could be more absurd than to believe that eighty thousand craftsmen had to ascend such a stair, to the narrow precincts of the Middle Chamber, to receive their wages in corn, wine, and in oil? Taken as an allegory, we see beauty in it, as it sets before us the picture of a Mason's duty,—to be ever on the search for knowledge, even though the steps in the attainment of it are winding and difficult ; but by study and perseverance we will gain our reward, and that reward more precious than either money, corn, oil, or wine—2 Chron. ii. 15.

Having passed into the Middle Chamber, the attention of Fellow Crafts is drawn to the letter G. or ‏י‎ placed conspicuous in the centre of it, to denote Geometry, the science on which this Degree is founded, but it refers more especially to G.˙.T.˙. G.˙.G.˙.O.˙.T.˙.U.˙.

CORN,	WINE,	OIL,
	Are emblematical of	
PLENTY,	CHEERFULNESS,	PEACE.

ARCHITECTURE.

Architecture is the art of building edifices, either for habitation or defence, and with respect to its objects, may be divided into three branches—Civil, Military, and Naval. Nature and necessity taught the first inhabitants of the earth to build huts to shelter them from the rigour of the seasons, and inclemency of the weather, which, in course of time, they improved ; and, after attaining what was useful and necessary, luxury and ambition caused them to ornament their buildings.

THE ORDERS OF ARCHITECTURE.

The Origin of the Orders of Architec'ure is almost as ancient as human society. At first the trunks of trees were set on end, while others were laid across to support the covering, hence, it is said, arose the idea of more regular architecture, the trees on end representing columns, the girts or bands which connected them express the bases and capitals, and the bressumers laid across gave the hint of entablatures, the coverings ending in points did of pediments. This is the hypothesis of Vitruvius. Others believe that columns took their rise from pyramids, which the ancients erected over their tombs, and the urns which enclosed the ashes of the dead represented the capitals, while a brick or stone laid thereon as a cover formed the abacus. The Greeks, however, were the first to regulate the height of their columns on the proportion of the human body, the Doric representing a strong man ; the Ionic, a woman ; and the Corinthian, a girl.

The various Orders took their names from the people among whom they were invented, and are thus classed—The Tuscan, Doric, Ionic, Corinthian, and Composite. Scamozzi uses significant terms to express their character ; he calls the Tuscan, the Gigantic; the Doric, the Herculean; the Ionic, the Matronal ; the Corinthian, the Virginal ; the Composite, the Heroic.

THE TUSCAN

Is the most simple and solid ; its column is seven diameters high, the capital, base, and entablature having few mouldings or ornaments.

THE DORIC

Is said to be the most ancient and best propor-
tioned of all the orders ; it has no ornaments on
base or capital except mouldings. The height
is eight diameters, and its frieze is divided by
Triglyphs and Metopes ; the oldest example ex-
tant is at Corinth.

THE IONIC

Bears a kind of mean proportion between the
more solid and delicate orders ; the capital is ornamented with volutes, and its cornice with denticles. The column is nine. diameters. Michael
Angelo gives it a single row of leaves at the bottom
of the capital.

THE CORINTHIAN

Is ten diameters high, and its capital is adorned
with two rows of leaves and eight volutes, which
sustain the abacus, and the cornice is ornamented
with denticles and modillions. Vitruvius relates
the following narrative of its invention :—" Calli-
machus, accidentally passing the tomb of a young
lady, he perceived a basket of toys, covered with
a tile, placed over an ancthus root, having been
left there by her nurse. As the branches grew up,
they encompassed the basket, till, arriving at the
tile, they met with an obstruction, and bent down-
wards. Struck with the beauty of the arrangement,
he set about imitating the figure, the basket representing the base of the capital ; the tile, the abacus ;
and the bending leaves, the volutes." ◄Foliated
capitals of much greater antiquity than any discovered in Greece, are, however, to be found in
Egypt and Asia Minor ; and Villalpandus says
" that it took its origin from an Order in Solo-

mon's Temple, the leaves whereof were those of the palm tree."

THE COMPOSITE

Is so called because it is composed of the other orders; the column is ten diameters high, and its cornice has denticles, or simple modillions.

There are, however, many other styles of architecture. The Teutonic is distinguished by semicircular arches, and massive plain columns.

The Gothic is distinguished by its lightness and profuse ornament, pointed arches, and pillars, carved so as to imitate several conjoined. The Egyptians, Chinese, Hindoos, Moors, &c., have each their own styles of ornamental buildings, and splendid specimens are to be seen in their several countries.

THE FIVE SENSES.

An analysis of the human faculties is next given in this Degree, in which the five external Senses particularly claim attention, as they are the root or foundation of all human knowledge. It will be seen, by a careful consideration of the functions of the Five Senses, that sensation and reflection are the great sources of human knowledge, and that they are the means by which all our first ideas and information are acquired, because external objects act first on our senses, and rouse us to a consciousness of their existence, and convey distinct impressions to the mind, according to the manner in which they affect us; the mind, storing up and remembering these impressions, assembles them, and compares one with another, and thus we acquire a new and more complex set of ideas, in which we observe variety, uniformity, similitude, symmetry, novelty, grandeur, and reference to an end ; and by the mind reflecting upon what passes within itself, creates another set of impressions no less distinct than those conveyed to it by the senses. Sensation is, therefore, the great source of human knowledge, and, at the same time, the boundary beyond which our conceptions cannot reach, for we are unable to find one original idea, which has not been derived from sensation. But we are not to conclude that, because solid and thinking beings are the only ideas of existence which we are able to form, that there may not be a class of beings superior to mankind, enjoying other powers of perception unknown to us ; we might as well conclude that the want of the ideas of light and colour, in a man born blind, would be an argument against the reality or possibility of their existence—

" *For though things sensible be numberless,*
  But only five the senses' organs be
And in those five, all things their forms express,
  Which we can touch, taste, smell, hear, or see."

THE EYE

Is the organ of Sight, and seeing is that sense by which we distinguish objects, forms, colours, motion, rest, and distance or space, &c.

" *The beams of light had been in vain displayed,*
  Had not the eye been fit for vision made ;
In vain the Author had the eye prepared
  With so much skill, had not the light appeared."

HEARING

Is the sense by which we distinguish sounds, and enjoy all the charms of music ; by it we are enabled to communicate with each other, and enjoy the pleasures of society, and avoid many dangers that we would otherwise be exposed to.

> *" Is there a heart that music cannot melt ?*
> *Alas ! how is that rugged heart forlorn !*
> *Is there who ne'er those mystic transports felt*
> *Of solitude and melancholy born ?"*

FEELING

Is the sense by which we acquire ideas of hardness and softness, roughness and smoothness, heat and cold, &c., and is the most universal of our senses.

These three senses are peculiarly essential to Masons, *i.e.*, to see the Signs, hear the Words, and feel the Grips.

TASTING

Is the sense by which we distinguish sweet from sour, bitter from salt, &c., and enables us to make a proper distinction in the choice of our food.

SMELLING

Is the sense by which we distinguish sweet, sour, aromatic, and fœtid or offensive odours, which convey different impressions to the mind ; and the design of the G∴A∴O∴T∴U∴ is manifest in having located the organ of smell in the nostrils, the channels through which the air is continually passing.

The inconceivable wisdom of the Almighty Being is displayed in the five senses. The structure of the mind, and all the active powers of the soul present a vast and boundless field for philosophical investigation, which far exceeds human inquiry;

and are peculiar mysteries, **known** only to Nature and to Nature's God, to whom **we are** indebted for every blessing **we** enjoy. This theme is therefore peculiarly worthy of attention.

The Seven Liberal Arts and Sciences are— Grammar, Logic, Rhetoric, Arithmetic, Geometry, Astronomy, and Music.

GRAMMAR

Embraces the whole science of language, and teaches us to express our ideas in appropriate words.

LOGIC

Is the art of correct thinking, and directs our inquiries after truth, by conceiving of things clearly and distinctly, thereby preventing us from being misled by similitude or sophistry.

RHETORIC

Is the art of speaking eloquently, in order to please, instruct, persuade, and command; and is by no means a common or an easy attainment.

ARITHMETIC

Is the science of numbers, and teaches us to compute or calculate correctly with expedition and ease.

GEOMETRY

Is the science of extension or magnitude, abstractedly considered, and treats of lines, surfaces, and solids; as all extension is distinguished by length, breadth, and thickness. A geometrical point has no parts, neither length, breadth, nor thickness, and is therefore indivisible. A line is

length without breadth, and a superficies is length
and breadth without thickness. The point is the
termination of the line, the line is the termination
of the superficies, and the superficies the termination of a body.

By this science, which is the foundation of
architecture, and the root of mathematics, man is
enabled to measure any place or distance, ac-
cessible or inaccessible, if it can only be seen.
By it geographers show us the magnitude of the
earth, the extent of seas, empires, and provinces,
&c. ; and by it astronomers are enabled to measure
the distance, motions, and magnitudes of the
heavenly bodies, and regulate the duration of
times, seasons, years, and cycles. Geometry is
particularly recommended to the attention of
Masons, not only as a study of lines, superficies,
and solids, but as a method of reasoning and
deduction in the investigation of truth, and may
be considered as a kind of natural logic. The contemplation of this science, in a moral and comprehensive view, fills the mind with rapture. The
flowers, the animals, the mountains, and every
particle of matter which surround us, open a
sublime field for inquiry, and proves the wisdom
of God, and the existence of a First Cause.

> "*I read His awful name, emblazon'd high,*
> *With golden letters, on the illumin'd sky;*
> *Nor less the mystic characters I see*
> *Wrought in each flower, inscribed on every tree;*
> *In every leaf that trembles on the breeze,*
> *I hear the voice of God among the trees.*"

ASTRONOMY

Is a mixed mathematical science, and the most
sublime that has ever been cultivated by man. It

treats of the celestial bodies, and affords an interesting theme for instruction and contemplation, kindling the mind to praise, love, and adore the Supreme Creator.

> " *How distant some of the nocturnal suns !*
> *So distant, says the sage, 'twere not absurd*
> *To doubt if beams, set out at Nature's birth,*
> *Are yet arrived at this so foreign world ;*
> *Though nothing half so rapid as their flight,*
> *An eye of awe and wonder let me roll,*
> *And roll for ever. Who can satiate sight*
> *In such a scene, in such an ocean wide*
> *Of deep astonishment? Where depth, height,*
>   *breadth,*
> *Are lost in their extremes ; and where, to count*
> *The thick-sown glories in this field of fire,*
> *Perhaps a seraph's computation fails.*"

MUSIC

Is the science of harmonious sounds, and is the effect of vibration, propagated like light, from atom to atom, and depending on the reflection of surrounding bodies and the density of the air.

> " *Of all the arts beneath the heaven*
> *That man has found, or God has given,*
> *None draws the soul so sweet away,*
> *As Music's melting, mystic lay ;*
> *Slight emblem of the bliss above,*
> *It soothes the spirit all to love.*"

THE CHARGE.

Being now advanced to the Second Degree of Masonry, we congratulate you on your preferment. As you increase in knowledge, you will improve in social intercourse. In your new character, it is

expected that you will conform to the principles
of the Order, by steadily persevering in the practice of every commendable virtue. You are not
to palliate or aggravate the offences of your
Brethren; but in the decision of every trespass
against our rules, you are to judge with candour,
admonish with friendship, and reprehend with
justice. The study of the liberal arts, which tends
to polish and adorn the mind, is earnestly recommended to your consideration, especially the
science of Geometry, which is enriched with useful knowledge; while it proves the wonderful
properties of nature, it demonstrates the more important truths of morality, which is the basis of
our art. We exhort you to strive, like a skilful
Brother, to excel in everything that is good and
great; and may you improve your intellectual
faculties, and qualify yourself to become a useful
member of society, and an ornament to the Craft.

As Moses was commanded to pull the shoes from off his feet, on Mount Horeb, because the ground on which he trod was sanctified by the presence of Divinity, so should a Mason advance to the Third Stage of Masonry, in the naked paths of Truth, with steps of innocence, virtue, and humility.

THE THIRD,

OR

MASTER MASONS' DEGREE,

Represents man saved from the Grave of Iniquity, and raised to Salvation, by faith and the grace of God. In this Degree we look beyond the narrow limits of this world to that celestial sphere—

> *" Where high the heavenly temple stands,*
> *The house of God not made with hands."*

By a proper study of this Degree, we are taught to

> *" Contemplate when the sun declines,*
> *Our death with deep reflection ;*
> *And when again he rising shines,*
> *Our day of resurrection."*

OPENING PRAYER.

Oh, thou all-seeing and omnipresent God, from everlasting to everlasting, we pray thee to direct us how to know and serve thee aright, and bow before thy throne of grace, for the forgiveness of our sins, that we may obtain fellowship with thee, and promote the honour and glory of thy most holy name.　Amen, so mote it be.

THE SANCTUM SANCTORUM.

A Master Mason's Lodge duly opened, represents the Sanctum Sanctorum, or Holy of Holies, of King Solomon's Temple, where not even kings are allowed to enter unless duly initiated, and raised to that high and sublime privilege, by the help of God, his good name, and the united aid of square and compasses, which represent

VIRTUE, MORALITY, FRIENDSHIP, and LOVE.

Having entered, in due form, a Master's Lodge, that beautiful passage of scripture (Eccl. xii. 1-7), representing the infirmities of old age, should always be remembered as an appropriate introduction to the sublime ceremonies of this Degree, and the lessons taught by our emblematic death, and resurrection to life eternal.

THE SYMBOLIC JEWELS

Of a Master Mason are Friendship, Morality, and Brotherly Love. These he should wear as an adornment to his mind—Morality being practical virtue, and the duty of life; Friendship is personal kindness, which should extend beyond the circle of private connections to universal philanthropy; and Brotherly Love is the purest emanation of earthly friendship.

THE WORKING TOOLS

Are the Skirret, the Pencil, Compasses, and all the implements of Masonry, especially

THE TROWEL,

Which emblematically teaches us to spread the cement of brotherly love, unite in one bond of social union, and diffuse the principle of universal benevolence to every member of the human family.

THE SKIRRET

Is emblematical of the straight and undeviating line of conduct, which directs us in the path which leads to immortality as revealed to us in the volume of the Sacred Law.

THE PENCIL

Reminds us that our words and actions are recorded by the Almighty Architect, to whom we must give an account of them, whenever it is his pleasure to call on us to do so.

THE COMPASSES

Peculiarly belong to this Degree, as when properly extended, they embrace all the tenets of the Order, limit our desires, and keep our passions within due bounds, so that we may, as Master Masons, lead a life of physical as well as moral and intellectual integrity.

HIRAM ABIFF.

Before proceeding further with the M.M. Degree, it will be necessary to give an outline of the historical, or rather allegorical, legend on which the most important part of this Degree is founded, as it is intended to symbolise our faith in the resurrection of the body, and the immortality of the soul, and gives an instance of firmness and fidelity to our duty in contrast with the cunning and deceitful passions which are so pernicious and destructive to all who indulge in them. To assume the story to be literally a historical fact instead of an allegory, would be to rob the impressive ceremony of its beauty, and weaken the effect which is intended to be produced by it on the mind.

The Bible informs us that a person, of the name of Hiram, was employed at the building of King Solomon's Temple (1 Kings vii. 13; 2 Chron, ii. 13-14); but neither the Bible, nor any other authority, except Masonic tradition, gives any further information respecting him, not even of his death; how it occurred, when, or where. According to the Masonic legend, it was the custom of Hiram, as Grand Master of the work, to enter the Sanctum Sanctorum every day at high twelve (when the workmen were called from labour to refreshment), to offer up prayers, and adore the

God in whom he put his trust. The Temple at length being nearly finished, and the Craftsmen not having obtained the Master's Word, which was only known to King Solomon, Hiram King of Tyre, and Hiram Abiff, fifteen of them conspired to extort it from him, or take his life, they being determined to have the Word by any means, so as to enable them to travel into foreign countries, and obtain employment. Twelve of them, however, repented, and confessed to King Solomon what they had conspired to do. It does not, however, appear that Solomon took any active steps to prevent the murder of Hiram, for we are told that when he arrived at the Temple, all was in confusion, and, on making inquiry as to the cause, he was informed that the Grand Master, Hiram Abiff, was missing, and that there were no plans on the trestle board for them to work by. Recollecting what had been confessed to him that morning, and knowing that Hiram had always been punctual and regular, he began to fear that some mischief had been done to him ; he then ordered the roll to be called, when three were found to be missing (namely, Jubela, Jubelo, and Jubelum). Solomon immediately caused an embargo to be laid on all the shipping, so as to prevent their escape to a foreign country, and ordered fifteen Fellow Crafts to be sent in search of the ruffians, and that if they could not be found, the twelve who had confessed were to be considered as the murderers, and suffer accordingly. Those who had been sent west, on coming near the coast of Joppa, heard voices issuing from a cavern in the rocks, and on listening, discovered that the desperadoes had been unable to obtain a passage to Ethiopia, or escape from their own country.

Jubela was first heard to exclaim, "Oh that my throat had been cut across, or my tongue torn out by the root, and my body buried in the sands of the sea at low water mark, ere I had been accessary to the death of our Grand Master!"

Jubelo next exclaimed, "Oh that my heart had been torn from my breast, and my body given to the wild beasts of the field and the vultures of the air, ere I had conspired to take the life of so good a man!!"

Jubelum, in his despair, cried, "Oh that my body had been severed in two, my bowels torn out, burnt to ashes, and scattered by the winds of heaven, so that there might not remain the least trace or remembrance of so vile a wretch as I, who struck the fatal blow, and caused the death of our Grand Master Hiram Abiff!!!" On hearing these exclamations, the searchers rushed suddenly upon them, took them prisoners, and conveyed them to Jerusalem, where they confessed their guilt, and were executed, each according to the sentence passed from his own lips. Fifteen Craftsmen were again assembled, and, clothed in white aprons and gloves in token of innocence, were sent, three East, three West, three North, three South, and three in and about the Temple, to search for the body of Hiram, which was discovered in an accidental manner, by one who became wearied and sat down to rest on the brow of a hill. On rising, he caught hold of a sprig of cassia, which easily gave way, and showed that the earth had been recently moved. He called for his companions, who came to his assistance, and discovered the body of their Master very indecently interred. With due respect they again covered the body, and hastened to acquaint King Solomon, who, on hearing the melancholy intelligence, raised his hands, and exclaimed "Oh Lord my God, is there no help for the widow's son," and dropped them in such a manner as indicated the grief into which he was thrown. Immediately recovering himself, he commanded the body to be raised and conveyed to Jerusalem, to be interred in a sepulchre, as near the Sanctum Sanctorum as the Jewish law would permit, in honour of his rank and exalted talents.

THE THREE RUFFIANS

In the foregoing allegory are typical of Deceit, (or the devil,) Avarice, and Death, who invaded man's original innocent state, and laid him prostrate in the grave of spiritual death.

The law came to his aid, but failed to raise his corruptible nature.

Idolatry offered her assistance, but also proved a *slip*, and failed to effect his moral resurrection.

At length the Gospel, "marked with the seal of high Divinity," descended from heaven, and pronounced the omnific word, which raised him from a spiritual death to everlasting life, robbed death of its sting, and swallowed it up in victory (Isaiah xxv. 8; 1 Cor. xv. 54-57). Thus a Master Mason represents man, saved from the grave of iniquity and corruption, and raised to the sphere of righteousness and salvation, where peace and innocence for ever dwell, in the realms of a boundless eternity.

THE MONUMENT

Erected to the memory of Hiram was a broken column of white marble supporting a book, with a virgin weeping over them. an urn in her left hand, and a sprig of acacia in her right. Time standing behind her with his fingers entwined in the ringlets of the virgin's hair.

THE BROKEN COLUMN

Is emblematical of the frailty of man, and all things human. " To everything there is a season, and a time to every purpose under the sun" (Eccl. chap. iii.).

THE OPEN BOOK

Is emblematical of the revealed will of God, and the Book of Nature, open for our investigation.

" *See through this air, this ocean, and this earth,*
All matter quick, and bursting into birth."

THE VIRGIN WEEPING OVER THEM

Beautifully illustrates the melancholy contemplation that "Thy doom is written, dust thou art, and shalt to dust return ;" for no sooner do we begin to live, than Death begins to follow us, borne on the wings of Time, whose scythe is ever cutting short our string of moments ; even now his fingers are entwined in our vitals, and will soon cut the brittle thread of life.

" *How loved, how valued once, avails thee not,*
To whom related, or by whom begot ;
A heap of dust alone remains for thee,
'Tis all thou art ! and all the proud shall be."

THE SPRIG OF ACACIA,

With its graceful drooping leaves, like the weeping willow, is an emblem of tender Sympathy and never-dying Affection, and being an evergreen, is also emblematical of the immortal Soul that never dies ; and this thought is calculated, in the hope of a glorious immortality, to dispel the gloomy contemplation and fear of death.

> " *Death cannot come*
> *To him untimely who is fit to die ;*
> *The less of this cold world, the more of heaven ;*
> *The briefer life, the earlier immortality.*"

THE FIVE POINTS OF FELLOWSHIP,

On which every Master Mason is raised from his emblematic death, are—

First, Hand in hand ; I will respect you as a brother, if I find you worthy.

Second, * * *; That I will travel through danger and difficulties to assist a fellow creature in distress, particularly a worthy Brother, if not detrimental to myself or connections.

Third, * * *; In my daily prayers to Almighty God, I will remember a Brother's welfare as my own.

Fourth. * * *; That a Brother's just and lawful secrets will I keep as my own, in the sacred repository of my heart.

Fifth, * * *; That I will support a Brother's character in his absence as I would in his presence. Thus are we linked together by the indissoluble chain of Affection, Relief, Truth, Justice, and Brotherly Love. . . . .

THE EMBLEMS

Particularly recommended to the attention of Master Masons inculcate many a useful lesson, as showing us how we may become examples in our religious, civil, and moral conduct.

THE MALLET

Is the emblem of Power, morally teaching us to correct irregularities, and reduce man to a proper level.

THE THREE STEPS

Are emblematical of the three Masonic Degrees, or stages of human life—viz., Youth, Manhood, and Old Age ; and also of the three periods of our existence—viz., Time, Death, and Eternity.

> " *What is the gift of Life*
> *To him who reads with heaven-instructed eye ?*
> *' Tis the first dawning of eternity ;*
> *The future heaven just breaking on the sight ;*
> *The glimmering of a still increasing light.*"

THE POT OF INCENSE

Is the emblem of a Pure Heart, glowing with fervent love, and ascending to heaven in perfumes of filial gratitude, like the cloud of celestial white that filled the Temple at Jerusalem,

> " *As though an angel in his upward flight,*
> *Had left his mantle floating in mid air.*"

4

THE BEEHIVE

Is an emblem of Industry. Idleness, which is the parent of immorality and ruin, is severely reproved by this symbol. By industry we may enjoy all the necessaries and even the luxuries of life, avoid vice and temptation, and merit respect, by adding knowledge to the understanding, so that we may not be considered a useless drone in the busy hive of nature.

THE BOOK OF CONSTITUTIONS,

GUARDED BY THE TYLER'S SWORD,

Should remind us to be guarded in our Thoughts, Words, and Actions ; for the Sword of Almighty Vengeance is drawn to reward iniquity.

THE SWORD POINTING TO A NAKED HEART

Reminds us that, although our thoughts and actions may be hid from the eyes of man, Justice will sooner or later overtake us. Let us, therefore, be ever ready to pass the Grim Tyler of Eternity without fear, when we are called upon to serve our Master in Heaven.

THE ALL-SEEING EYE

Of the Incomprehensible, Omnipotent God ! whose being extends through boundless space, and "penetrates the very inmost recesses of subterranean cells," must see and know our Thoughts and Actions, and will reward us according to our merits.

THE FORTY-SEVENTH PROBLEM OF EUCLID.

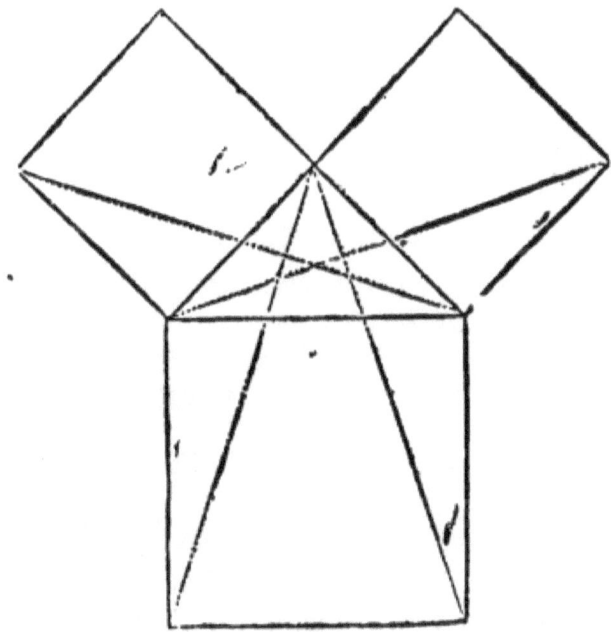

Theorem. In any right angled triangle, the square described upon the side subtending the right angle is equal to the squares described upon the sides which contain the right angle.

This problem, which is of great use in geometrical solutions and demonstrations of quantities, is said to be the invention of the philosopher Pythagoras, and which, in the joy of his heart, he called Eureka (I have found it), and sacrificed a hecatomb to commemorate the discovery. It is emblematical of the symmetry and beauty of Creation, and the unalterable laws of Divine wisdom and infinite power which govern every atom of the universe. It should remind Masons that they ought to love and study the arts and sciences.

THE ARK

Is an emblem of Safety, and our trust in God, to waft us securely o'er the tempestuous sea of life to that harbour where—

> " *From every snare and evil work*
>   *His grace shall us defend,*
> *And to his heavenly kingdom safe*
>   *Shall bring us in the end.*"

THE ANCHOR

Is the emblem of a well grounded Hope in a Glorious Immortality, when moored for ever to that shore, where "The wicked cease from troubling, and the weary are at rest."

THE HOUR GLASS

Is an emblem of Human Life. The sand in the glass passes swiftly, though almost imperceptibly, away. So do the moments of our lives, till the wave of Time is swallowed up by the billows of Eternity.

> " *What are our ages but a few brief waves*
>   *From the vast ocean of Eternity,*
> *That break upon the shores of this our world,*
> *And so ebb back into the immense profound.*"

> " *Emblem of life! which, still as we survey,*
> *Seems motionless, yet ever glides away.*"

THE SCYTHE

Is the emblem of Time, which cuts the brittle thread of life, and launches us into eternity.

> " *Redeem thine hours—the space is brief—*
>   *While in thy glass the sand grains shiver ;*
> *And measureless thy joy or grief,*
>   *When Time and thou shalt part for ever.*"

THE SPADE

I% an emblem reminding us that "All nature dies and lives again," and that this world is but the tilling ground of heaven, to cultivate our morals and improve in knowledge, so as to strengthen our faith, look beyond the grave, and rely on the grace of God to raise our living souls to the regions of everlasting blessedness.

> " *Haste, seize the proffered hope of heaven,*
> *While life and light are yet thine own ;*
> *Swift as the passing cloud of even,*
> *Time glides along—and thou art gone.*"

THE COFFIN, SKULL, AND CROSS-BONES

Are emblems of the inevitable destiny of our Mortal Bodies. The grave yawns to receive us:

> " *And creeping things shall revel in their spoil,*
> *And fit our clay to fertilise the soil.*"

> " *The grave, that never spoke before,*
> *Hath found at length a tongue to chide ;*
> *Oh listen ! I will speak no more—*
> *Be silent Pride !*"

THE SPRIG OF ACACIA

Is an emblem of Immortality. (See page 46).

> " *The dead are like the stars by day*
> *Withdrawn from mortal eye,*
> *But not extinct, they hold their way*
> *In glory through the sky.*"

> " *Spirits from bondage thus set free,*
> *Vanish amidst immensity,*
> *Where human thought, like human sight,*
> *Fails to pursue their trackless flight.*"

THE ORNAMENTS

Of this Degree are the Porch, the Chequered Pavement, and the Dormer, or Window.

THE PORCH,

Or Entrance to the Holy of Holies, will remind the thoughtful Master Mason of his emblematic death, and that the grave is the Porch which all must pass through to the world of spirits, where worthy servants only will find admittance to the Sanctum Sanctorum of that Celestial Lodge where the Grand Master of the Universe presides.

THE CHEQUERED PAVEMENT

For the High Priest to walk on, and burn incense on the golden altar, praying the Almighty for prosperity and peace, is emblematical of the alternative, or choice between two things, *i.e.*, Good or Evil, Light or Darkness, Pleasure or Pain, Heaven or Hell; for " ye cannot serve God and Mammon, if ye reject one, ye must take the other."

" *When beneath to their darkness the wicked are driven,*
May our justified souls find a welcome in heaven."

THE DORMER,

Or Window, which gives light to the Sanctum Sanctorum, is emblematical of the Fountain of Wisdom, which enlightens the mind, and dispels the gloomy darkness of ignorance, and instructs us how to die.

" *Grant that in life's last hour my soul may crave,*
Nor crave in vain, his love to light me through the
grave."

CHARGE FOR THE **THIRD** DEGREE.

Brother,—As you are now raised to the High
and Sublime Degree of a Master Mason, I would
ask you to take a retrospective glance at the various
Degrees and Ceremonies which you have passed
through, and would exhort you to study and practise the moral precepts therein laid down.   In the
First Degree, youth is represented as ignorant and
blind, groping in mental darkness for intellectual
light, which darkness can only be dispelled by
years of study and experience, before its beams
can illuminate the mind.

We are also reminded that, in the sight of God,
all mankind are equal, by entering the world naked
from the womb, and so returning back to our
mother earth (Job i. 21), leaving wealth and titles,
honour and power, behind us, as worthless baubles,
of no value or avail to purchase place or happiness
in the world to come.   For this reason you were
taught to have faith in God, hope in immortality,
and to be charitable to all mankind.   Charity, you
are to remember, is the chief of every social virtue,
and ought to be the distinguishing characteristic of
every Mason ; yet, even with charity, it is necessary to be cautious, for it is an error to dispense
alms indiscriminately.to all supplicants, whereby
the hypocrite and knave may eat the bread which
virtue in distress ought to be relieved by.   Charity
is often abused, for there are many miscreants who
infest our streets and doors with their importuni-
ties, many even showing their sores and distorted
bodies, to prompt a false compassion, with which

ill-gotten gains they revel away the hours of night in debauchery. Charity, when misapplied, loses the dress of virtue and assumes the garb of folly; therefore, let the bounties of your benevolence be ruled by discretion, and bestowed on such objects as Merit and Virtue in distress, Innocence in tears, Widows and Orphans left helpless on the world, Old age, and Industrious persons whom misfortune has overtaken and reduced to poverty and want; for, if angels in heaven weep, it is for the pangs of poverty and want which rend the hearts of the deserving poor; therefore, we beseech you not to withhold your mite or assistance when in your power to relieve distress, or soothe the unhappy (1 Cor. xii. 1). Study God in nature, and there you will see Wisdom, Strength, and Beauty in all his works as pillars supporting the great temple of the universe. In the Second Degree, you see Manhood labouring to overcome the difficulties which beset him in the pursuit of knowledge, and thus the intellectual faculties are employed in promoting the glory of God, and the good of man. In the high and sublime Degree of a Master Mason, you are taught to look beyond the narrow limits of this world, and see man raised from the grave of iniquity, by Faith and the grace of God, to Everlasting life and Blessedness. Let us, therefore, study our emblems, and practise their precepts, so that we may, as children of light, turn our backs on works of Darkness, Obscenity, Drunkenness, and all manner of evil, and live as we ought, practising Charity, Benevolence, Justice, Temperance, Chastity, and Brotherly Love.

CONCLUSION.

Having thus given a general summary of the

Masonic System of Morality, let us hope that it will be more than ever esteemed, and valued with increased reverential regard, by all who have traced the Royal Art from the commencement of the First to the end of the Third Degree.

According to the plan of Masonry, the mirror is as it were held up to Nature, that we may review the helplessness of our Youth, the vanity of the World, and the Trust we ought to put in God ; that the " Reflected Rays" from the Mirror may determine us to pursue such knowledge, and practise those virtues and precepts which will secure the respect of every true Mason and the approbation of all good men.

> " *Genius of Masonry descend,*
>   *And with thee bring thy spotless train ;*
>   *Constant our sacred rites attend,*
>   *While we adore thy peaceful reign.*"

Annually, Roan, Gilt Edges, Elastic Band,
PRICE TWO SHILLINGS.

THE

COSMOPOLITAN

Masonic Calendar,

DIARY, & POCKET BOOK.

Post Free, England, Ireland and Scotland, 2/2.
Foreign Parts, 8 oz. Book Post must be added.

IT CONTAINS

Lists of Lodges, Chapters, Conclaves, Grand Councils, and K.T. Preceptories, with the names of Officers in England and Wales, Scotland, Ireland, France, Belgium, Germany, Italy, Denmark, Portugal, Sweden and Norway, Greece, Turkey, New Brunswick, Venezuela, Netherlands, British Columbia, Peru, Quebec, Canada, America, &c.

The London Meetings of every Degree are given in the Memorandum space of each day. The Country Lodges appear in Towns, alphabetically arranged. It also contains the Charge and Entered Apprentice's Song.

OFFICE:—198, FLEET STREET, LONDON.

THE

LIFE OF CONSTANTINE

WRITTEN IN GREEK

By EUSEBIUS PAMPHILUS

(Bishop of Cæsarea in Palestine).

Done into English from that Edition set forth by
VALESIUS and printed in Paris in the year 1659.

PREFACE BY

BROS. R. WENTWORTH LITTLE, TREAS.
GEN., AND THE REV. A. F. A. WOODFORD,
Past Grand Chaplain.

WITH

Engravings of Constantine; The Duke of Sussex,
P.G. Sov. ; Lord Rancliffe, P.G. Sov. ; Earl
Bective M.P., P.G. Sov. ; Sir Fredk. Martin
Williams, Bart., M.P., M.G., Sov. ; &c., &c.

LONDON:
GEORGE KENNING, 198, FLEET STREET